PHARLANE CHONTAE LAOIS

MY FIRST BRITANNICA

The Arts

3

ENCYCLOPÆDIA
Britannica®

CHICAGO LONDON NEW DELHI PARIS SEOUL SYDNEY TAIPEI TOKYO

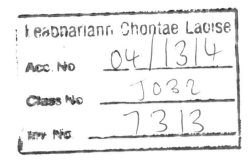
International Standard Book Number: 1-59339-048-3 (set)
International Standard Book Number: 1-59339-051-3 (volume 3)

My First Britannica:
Volume 3: The Arts 2004

Britannica.com may be accessed on the Internet at http://www.britannica.com.

The Arts

TABLE OF CONTENTS

Kermit the Frog

INTRODUCTION

Where did jazz come from? When did films begin to talk?
What do you call a musical play?
Who was Basho and what's a *haiku*?

In Volume 3,
The Arts,
you'll discover answers to these questions and many more. Through pictures, articles, and fun facts, you'll learn about the many kinds of art and meet some of the greatest artists of yesterday and today.

To help you on your journey, we've provided the following signposts in *The Arts*:

■ **Subject Tabs**—The coloured box in the upper corner of each right-hand page will quickly tell you the article subject.

■ **Search Lights**—Try these mini-quizzes before and after you read the article and see how much - *and how quickly* - you can learn. You can even make this a game with a reading partner. (Answers are upside down at the bottom of one of the pages.)

■ **Did You Know?**—Check out these fun facts about the article subject. With these surprising 'factoids', you can entertain your friends, impress your teachers, and amaze your parents.

■ **Picture Captions**—Read the captions that go with the photos. They provide useful information about the article subject.

■ **Vocabulary**—New or difficult words are in **bold type**. You'll find them explained in the Glossary at the back of this volume. And there's a complete listing of all Glossary terms in the set in the **Reference Guide and Index**, Volume 13.

■ **Learn More!**—Follow these pointers to related articles throughout the set.

And don't forget: If you're not sure where to start, where you saw something before, or where to go next, the **Reference Guide and Index** (Volume 13) will point the way.

Have a great trip!

MY FIRST BRITANNICA

Traditions of Creativity

Most of us have been to museums that display art by famous painters and sculptors. But another sort of artwork is common to almost every culture - the arts and crafts of non-famous but skilled people who carry on the traditions of their ancestors.

Folk art has its name because it's made by the 'folk', or common people, rather than by professional artists. Farmers, shepherds, fisher folk,

Hand-painted eggs from Ukraine, in eastern Europe.
© Craig Aurness/Corbis

and tradespeople who live away from cities are often the creators of folk art. Some are very skilled. European sailors used to carve beautiful scrimshaw - delicately engraved pieces of whalebone or **ivory**. Today, people in India, Ghana, Indonesia, and other places make beautiful fabrics in patterns unique to their regions.

In less **industrialized** countries in Asia, Africa, and Latin America, many folk arts and crafts are exported, and craftspeople can often make a living from them. Many of these countries support their craftspeople, usually by helping them to sell their work.

Folk artists typically produce useful things such as furniture, toys, jewellery, clothing, musical instruments, weapons, religious symbols, and household tools. They craft these objects from easy-to-find or **recycled** materials such as wire, wood, and natural **fibres**. Some people even make food into art.

Every region of the world has produced folk art in unique styles. Folk art frequently reflects the traditional wisdom, religious beliefs, and **superstitions** of a society. The art often focuses on important yet common events - births, marriages, funerals, and holidays.

SEARCH LIGHT

★

What material is used to make scrimshaw?

LEARN MORE! READ THESE ARTICLES...
FOLK MUSIC (VOLUME 3) • MYTHS AND LEGENDS, FOLKTALES AND FABLES (VOLUME 5) • SCULPTURE (VOLUME 3)

Native American Hopi artists carve kachina dolls, representing spirits of ancestors. Children learn about the kachina spirits while they play with the dolls.
© Tom Bean/Corbis

Answer: Scrimshaw uses whalebone or ivory as a surface for carvings.

Art of the Mind's Eye

A painting is a two-dimensional, or flat, work of visual art. It is created by applying some form of colour or paint to a surface.

Some artists paint what they see around them. Others paint pictures that they see in their imagination. The idea on which a painting is based is called its 'theme'.

Some paintings have a religious theme. For example, one of the most famous paintings in the world, Leonardo da Vinci's 'Last Supper', shows Jesus Christ sharing his final meal with his disciples.

Other paintings show famous legends and events in history. Or they show **landscapes**, animals, or even scenes from daily life. Many Chinese scroll paintings take landscapes and nature as their themes.

Artists also paint portraits, or pictures of people. Sometimes they paint pictures of themselves. Such paintings are called 'self-portraits'.

(Left) Navajo man making a sand painting. (Right) Classroom artist-in-training.

Some painters express ideas and feelings through lines, shapes, colours, and textures that don't look like anything you could recognize. Such paintings are called '**abstract** paintings'.

Painters use many materials in their work. These include oil paints, **acrylics,** watercolours, **pastels**, inks, dyes, and enamel paints. Painters use different tools to apply these colours, like brushes of various sizes and flexible tools called 'palette knives'.

You probably know that many paintings are made on canvas or paper. But paintings can also be applied to different surfaces. Murals are paintings on walls, both indoors and outdoors. Frescoes are wall paintings made on wet plaster. And some American Indians paint without paint in an art known as 'sand painting'.

In Islamic countries and in East Asia, especially Japan, Korea, and China, the art of beautiful writing, which is called 'calligraphy', is considered a skill equal to painting. Calligraphy is usually done in ink, using a brush.

LEARN MORE! READ THESE ARTICLES…
VINCENT VAN GOGH (VOLUME 3) • PABLO PICASSO (VOLUME 4)
XIA GUI (VOLUME 3)

Young artist works on a painting in a public exhibit at the Palace of Fine Arts in Santiago, Chile.
© Pablo Corral V/Corbis

SEARCH LIGHT

Find and correct the mistake in the following sentence: Calligraphy is a self-portrait done in ink.

The 3-D Art

Fill in the gaps: Sculpture is different from painting. A painting is _____, but a sculpture is _____-_____.

Sculpture is a **three-dimensional** visual art. Paintings, drawings, and photographs are all two-dimensional, or flat. Sculptures are most often shaped by carving, moulding, or **welding** materials.

Classical bronze sculpture by Donatello of Italian military figure Gattamelata.
© Elio Ciol/Corbis

Some are formed by making a cast - that is, by pouring a liquid into a mould and letting it harden.

Sculpture, like other arts, is often made to express thoughts or feelings. People who look at it might respond with thoughts or feelings of their own. Because it can have shape and **texture**, sculpture may appeal to our sense of touch.

Some sculptures are realistic. Until the middle of the 20th century, most sculpture was meant to look like some person or thing. The giant stone faces on Easter Island, like much traditional sculpture, may have been meant to honour gods or heroes. Other famous realistic sculptures include Michelangelo's 'David' and Auguste Rodin's 'The Thinker'.

Some modern sculptures may be **abstract**. This means they only hint at an object or an idea. They may not look like people or things you would recognize. These sculptures try to communicate a pure feeling or idea.

Sculptures come in all sizes, shapes, textures, and materials. Sculptors may use soft materials such as clay, wax, or wood or harder materials such as stone or metal. Sometimes the materials aren't even meant to last. One artist makes sculptures out of milk!

The modern sculptor Alexander Calder made sculptures that hang in the air. He called these 'mobiles' which means 'moving things'. Another modern sculptor, named Christo, makes sculptures by wrapping such things as bridges, buildings, and even small islands in fabric and plastic.

LEARN MORE! READ THESE ARTICLES…
FOLK ARTS AND CRAFTS (VOLUME 3) • MICHELANGELO (VOLUME 3)
AUGUSTE RODIN (VOLUME 3)

Modern sculpture, such as Claes Oldenburg's 'Clothespin' (in Philadelphia, Pennsylvania, U.S.), often places common objects in unusual situations to make us see and think about them differently.
© Robert Holmes/Corbis

Answer: Sculpture is different from painting. A painting is flat, but a sculpture is three-dimensional.

11

SEARCH LIGHT

Fill in
the gap:
Architecture is
the art of
_____.

The architect of the Baha'i House of Worship in India designed it to look like India's national flower. It has thus come to be called the Lotus Temple. Fine architecture is in tune with its cultural environment.
© Dallas and John Heaton/Corbis

The Art of Building

Thousands of years ago, early human beings lived in caves or other natural shelters. As time passed, people learned new skills, developed new tools, and were able to build simple structures.

As societies developed, they needed more kinds of building. Soon forts, barns, schools, bridges, tombs, and temples were being built, using a variety of materials. Gradually, creating buildings became an activity for experts - an art and occupation that came to be known as 'architecture'.

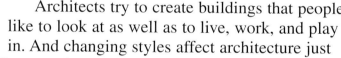

The Cathedral of Notre-Dame de Paris (begun in 1163), an example of Gothic architecture.
© Bill Ross/Corbis

Today architecture is a **refined** art requiring a lot of training, years of practice, and plenty of talent. An architect's work is to imagine and plan a building and then to supervise its construction.

The architect must keep many things in mind. For example, how is the building going to be used and by whom? Where will it be located? What would be the best materials to use? How much money will construction cost?

Architects try to create buildings that people like to look at as well as to live, work, and play in. And changing styles affect architecture just as happens in other arts. The next time you see or walk around a city, notice the various styles of building. You'll find many differences between those designed recently and those of even 50 or 100 years ago. Different countries and cultures also produce different styles of architecture.

People today are still amazed at the buildings created by long-ago architects. The **majestic** pyramids in Egypt, the Great Wall of China, the temple at Angkor Wat in Cambodia, and the Taj Mahal in India are some of the architectural wonders you can study and visit.

LEARN MORE! READ THESE ARTICLES...
HASSAN FATHY (VOLUME 3) • I.M. PEI (VOLUME 4) • TAJ MAHAL (VOLUME 7)

The Sadat Resthouse (built in Garf Huseyn, Egypt, in 1981) shows some of Hassan Fathy's trademark features. Here you can see the thick walls and air scoops that help cool the building naturally.

DID YOU KNOW?

Hassan Fathy is quoted as having said: 'Architecture is music frozen in place and music is architecture frozen in time.' What do you think he meant by this?

Home-style Architect

Hassan Fathy is famous as a **humanitarian** architect. He built homes and buildings that put people's needs first. Fathy was born in 1900 in Alexandria, Egypt. He studied there and began his career in Egypt.

Fathy's goal was to build **affordable** housing for local Egyptian people. He felt that many European building methods and designs that had come into his country were not well suited to it. He thought houses should be built from local materials, according to local designs, and with traditional methods. By building in this way he lowered the cost of his houses and respected the culture of the area as well. In addition, traditional methods and materials tended to suit the local climate best.

Because Egypt is a very hot country, it is important to plan houses that are as cool as possible. Fathy's buildings often had thick walls (to keep out the heat) surrounding an interior courtyard. Air scoops on the roof caught winds from the desert and funnelled them down through the buildings. By these methods, Fathy managed to cool his buildings naturally.

SEARCH LIGHT

The New Gourna Village was built from
a) sticks.
b) straw.
c) mud.

Hassan Fathy.
Courtesy of the Aga Khan Trust for Culture

One of Fathy's most famous creations was the New Gourna Village near Luxor, Egypt. The original village was near the **archaeological** digs of ancient Luxor and had to be relocated. Fathy trained the local people in the ancient tradition of mud brick construction. The people then built homes for themselves that were made almost entirely from mud bricks and that kept all the good features of their former homes.

Fathy died in 1989, but his work has inspired many young architects in the Middle East. He promoted ideas that adapted traditional styles and methods to the needs of the present day.

LEARN MORE! READ THESE ARTICLES...
ARCHITECTURE (VOLUME 3) • EGYPT (VOLUME 8) • I.M. PEI (VOLUME 4)

Answer: c) mud.

This painting, called 'Festival Day', is from Hiroshige's Tokaido Road series. In it, holiday travellers climb to a restaurant perched on a scenic lookout.

Artist of the Floating World

Ando Hiroshige was a Japanese painter and printmaker who was especially famous for his pictures of landscapes. Hiroshige was one of the *ukiyo-e* painters. '*Ukiyo-e*' is a Japanese term that means 'pictures of the floating world'.

Hiroshige was born in 1797. When he was 14, Hiroshige joined the school of the *ukiyo-e* master Utagawa Toyohiro. He graduated as an artist from the school at only 15. His first work was published six years later, in 1818.

Hiroshige probably created more than 5,000 **prints** during his lifetime. His life as an artist was divided into three stages. The first stage was when he was a student. He followed the style of his teachers in making prints of people. He drew girls, actors, and **samurai**, or warriors.

During the second stage Hiroshige made **landscape** designs and prints of birds and flowers. His best works during this time were 55 landscape prints called the 'Fifty-three Stations of the Tokaido'. Tokaido was a road that connected the Japanese cities of Osaka, Kyoto, and Edo (now called Tokyo). Along the road were 53 towns. Inns in each town provided lodging, food, and gifts for travellers. Hiroshige made one print for each town, as well as one each for the beginning of the road and the arrival in Kyoto. Many people bought copies of the prints. Hiroshige was soon one of the most popular *ukiyo-e* artists of all time.

In the last stage of his work, Hiroshige illustrated more landscapes, some empty and some with people in them. But he did far too much work, and his later work wasn't his best.

It has been estimated that Hiroshige created more than 5,000 prints. He knew how to create very simply and beautifully what he saw.

SEARCH LIGHT

What important road was the subject of many of Hiroshige's paintings?

LEARN MORE! READ THESE ARTICLES...
BASHO (VOLUME 3) • JAPAN: MODERN NATION OF
ANCIENT TRADITIONS (VOLUME 7) • XIA GUI (VOLUME 3)

DID YOU KNOW?
The Tokaido Road had been in use for over 700 years when Hiroshige began to make pictures of it.

Answer: Hiroshige was famous for his pictures of stops along the Tokaido Road.

17

SEARCH LIGHT

Frida Kahlo's most famous paintings were
a) murals.
b) self-portraits.
c) buses.

The Brilliant Colours of Mexico

Mexican painter Frida Kahlo's life was filled with struggles. But her dazzlingly colourful **self-portraits** reflect Kahlo's power and confidence in the face of her hardships.

When Kahlo was a child she had polio, and the disease kept her right leg from growing properly. Then, when she was 18, Kahlo was in a terrible bus accident. For the rest of her life she had many operations to try to correct both of these problems.

Kahlo began to paint while she was recovering from the bus accident. Her paintings were often dramatic self-portraits that showed Kahlo's powerful feelings about herself and the world she lived in. Their brilliant colours reflect Kahlo's bold attitude toward life.

Before the bus accident, Kahlo had met the famous Mexican painter Diego Rivera while he was painting a **mural** at her school. Later she showed Rivera some of her paintings and he encouraged her to keep working at her art.

Kahlo and Rivera were married in 1929. They travelled to the United States where Rivera had received **commissions** for murals. Kahlo kept painting and met many important people of the time. The artist Pablo Picasso admired her work. And many of her well-known friends helped her show her paintings in Europe and America.

Kahlo's work was called 'surrealistic' by some. Surrealism is a style of art that has a strange dreamlike quality. Kahlo, however, said that her paintings were the reality that she felt and that they spanned both reality and dreams.

In the spring of 1953 Kahlo had the only exhibition of her work in Mexico. She died one year later. Today her house in Coyoacán is the Frida Kahlo Museum.

LEARN MORE! READ THESE ARTICLES…
MEXICO (VOLUME 9) • PAINTING (VOLUME 3)
DIEGO RIVERA (VOLUME 3)

Frida Kahlo was the first Hispanic woman to be featured on a U.S. postage stamp. The stamp, seen here being unveiled, featured one of her famous self-portraits.
© AFP/Corbis

DID YOU KNOW?
Kahlo was very proudly Mexican. She often wore very decorative Mexican jewellery and native clothing. Her hairstyle, piled high on her head, was also in the style of the people of the Mexican state of Oaxaca.

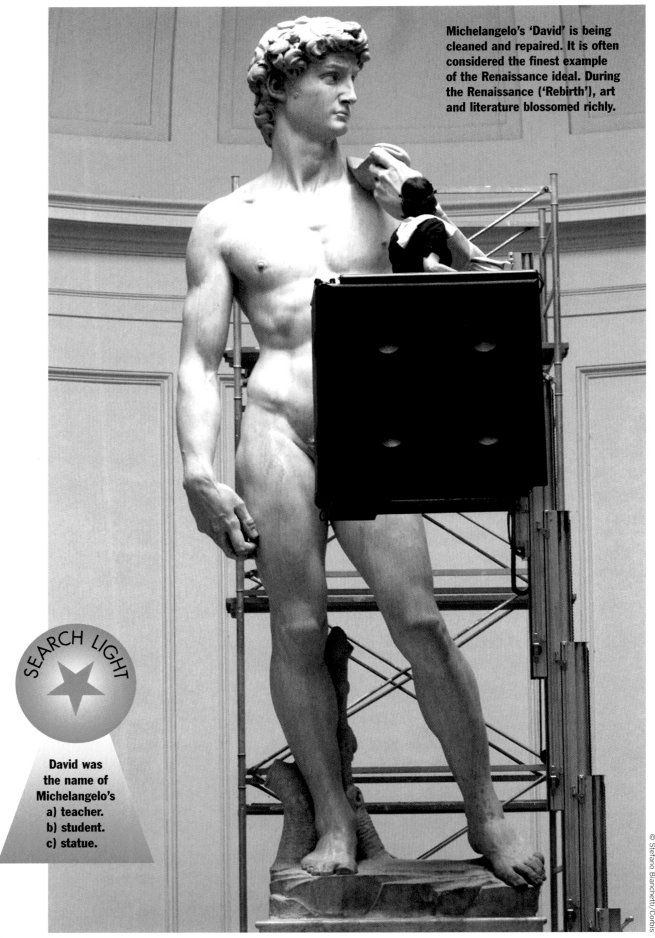

Michelangelo's 'David' is being cleaned and repaired. It is often considered the finest example of the Renaissance ideal. During the Renaissance ('Rebirth'), art and literature blossomed richly.

SEARCH LIGHT

David was the name of Michelangelo's
a) teacher.
b) student.
c) statue.

Genius of European Art

Once there was a small boy in Florence who loved to watch painters and sculptors at work. He wanted to be an artist, but his father did not like the idea. Little did the man know that his son Michelangelo would become one of the world's most famous artists.

Michelangelo began training as an artist at age 13. He was so interested in his art that he often forgot to eat and slept on the floor beside his unfinished artwork. He refused help, even on big projects, so some works took years to complete. Many were never finished.

Michelangelo worked in Rome and Florence. In Rome he was **commissioned** to carve a Pietà. This is a

(Top) Portrait of Michelangelo. (Bottom) Michelangelo's frescoes on the Sistine Chapel ceiling and west wall (behind the altar).

marble statue showing the Virgin Mary supporting the dead Christ on her knees. The finished work, known as the 'Madonna della Pietà', made him famous. And in Florence, Michelangelo spent two years working on a huge block of marble. From it he carved 'David', one of the world's finest and best-known sculptures.

Between 1508 and 1512 Michelangelo created his most famous work, the paintings on the ceiling of the Sistine Chapel in the Vatican in Rome. He painted much of the ceiling lying on his back in a tight cramped position. The **fresco** paintings of figures and events from the Bible are huge and splendid. The wall behind the altar **depicts** the Last Judgment of humanity by God.

Michelangelo was so admired that he became the first European artist whose life story was written during his own lifetime.

LEARN MORE! READ THESE ARTICLES...
BIBLE (VOLUME 5) • SCULPTURE (VOLUME 3)
VATICAN CITY (VOLUME 6)

DID YOU KNOW?
Despite all the time that went into his artwork, Michelangelo found time to design buildings, write poems, and even create defensive structures for Florence.

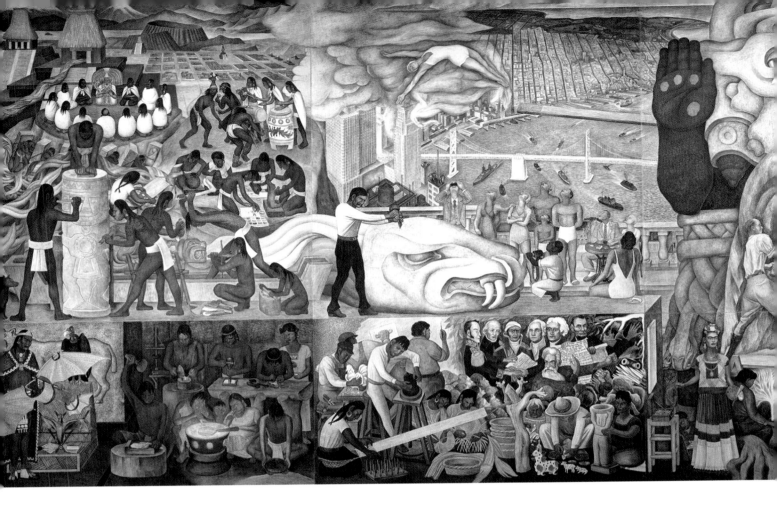

Murals of Mexico

When he was only 10 years old, Diego Rivera received a government scholarship to study art at the Academy of San Carlos in Mexico City. This would be the beginning of a brilliant career as an artist.

Later, Rivera studied in Spain, and in 1909 he moved to Paris. There he became friends with important painters such as Pablo Picasso and Georges Braque. While in France, Rivera began using simple forms and bold colours in his paintings.

Rivera returned to Mexico in 1921 after meeting fellow Mexican painter David Alfaro Siqueiros. The two shared a goal. They decided to create a new, uniquely Mexican kind of art based on **revolutionary** themes. They wanted this art to decorate public buildings, so they decided to paint murals. Murals are paintings done on walls, on either the inside or the outside of buildings. Rivera painted his first important mural,

> ### DID YOU KNOW?
> The owners of Rockefeller Center in New York City destroyed Rivera's mural there because it featured communist leader Vladimir I. Lenin. That mural would now be worth millions. Rivera later painted a copy in Mexico City.

Like many of Rivera's murals, this one focuses on the life and labours of the working class. This mural, called 'Pan American Unity', is painted on a wall at City College of San Francisco.

Which of the following qualities applies to Rivera's work?
a) bold colours
b) quiet pictures
c) pale colours

'Creation', for the National Preparatory School in Mexico City.

Rivera's many murals in his home country celebrated Mexican history and life. His paintings featured native Indians, Spanish **conquistadores**, Mexican peasants, factory workers, and famous philosophers, politicians, and other public figures. He liked to show how farming, industry, and culture were all connected in people's lives. His human figures had a flattened appearance and were outlined to emphasize their shape. His works were brightly coloured and crowded with figures, which made his huge murals seem even larger.

Rivera was in the United States from 1930 to 1934. There he painted murals for the California School of Fine Arts in San Francisco, the Detroit Institute of Arts, and Rockefeller Center in New York City.

Rivera's wife, Frida Kahlo, was also an important painter.

LEARN MORE! READ THESE ARTICLES...
FRIDA KAHLO (VOLUME 3) • MEXICO (VOLUME 9) • PABLO PICASSO (VOLUME 4)

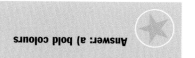

Answer: a) bold colours

The Modern Michelangelo

The French sculptor Auguste Rodin was interested in art even as a boy. At age 10 he started drawing. By the time he was 15, Rodin had discovered the art of **sculpture**.

Rodin started out working for building decorators. He did decorative stonework on the outside of buildings. Later, Rodin became a sculptor's assistant. He worked with the sculptor A.-E. Carrier-Belleuse.

In 1864, at age 24, Rodin publically showed his first major sculpture, 'The Man with the Broken Nose'. The official art **critics** of the time did not like it. They believed art should be about beauty. To them, Rodin's sculpture was about something 'ugly' and ordinary.

At age 35, Rodin went to Italy to study the work of the famous painter Michelangelo. He learned a great deal about the human form. His work began to look even more realistic. It seemed to be full of movement and drama.

When he was 37 years old, Rodin sculpted 'The Age of Bronze'. It was so unusual and realistic that people said he must have moulded it on a real person! After years of struggle Rodin finally had become known as a great sculptor.

Rodin's sculptures were usually **cast** in bronze or carved from marble. The bronze pieces could be duplicated many times, using an original piece that was moulded in clay.

The sculpture that Rodin is probably best known for is his statue 'The Thinker', shown in the photo here. Like almost all of his sculptures, it shows a person in a natural, everyday pose. But Rodin's work seems to show a reality and truth that people may not have noticed before. Many people still find that his work **symbolizes** the things that we all experience and feel.

DID YOU KNOW?

One of Rodin's most important sculptures, 'The Gates of Hell', was actually used as the doors of an art museum. Within it are many smaller sculptures. Many of them were early versions of what became some of Rodin's finest works.

SEARCH LIGHT

Fill in the gaps: The officials who studied and judged art felt that Rodin's first major work was _____ and _____.

LEARN MORE! READ THESE ARTICLES...
FRANCE (VOLUME 6) • MICHELANGELO (VOLUME 3)
SCULPTURE (VOLUME 3)

Answer: The officials who studied and judged art felt that Rodin's first major work was ugly and ordinary.

Sunflowers and Starry Nights

Vincent van Gogh was a Dutch artist of the 19th century and is now considered to be one of the greatest painters in the world. Van Gogh painted what he saw around him - trees, flowers, people, and buildings. He visited museums and met with other painters. But van Gogh had his own way of painting. He said he 'wanted to look at nature under a brighter sky.'

Self-portrait of van Gogh, painted in 1889.
© Archivo Iconografico, S.A./Corbis

In van Gogh's paintings, the southern French town of Arles is like no other place in the world. The skies are bluer and the sun is brighter. The orchards in bloom are pinker and greener. The cobblestone streets are more cobbled and stony. His pictures seem to be flooded with a golden light.

Van Gogh wanted wonderful colour in his pictures. His paintings called 'Sunflowers', 'Irises', and 'Starry Night' are among the most famous pictures he painted and are filled with brilliant colours. He tried to keep to the outward appearance of his subjects, yet his feelings about them exploded in strong colour and bold lines.

Van Gogh's style was direct, forceful, and natural. He worked with great speed and excitement. He was set on capturing an effect or a mood while it possessed him. He told his brother that if anyone said a painting was done too quickly, 'you can reply that they have looked at it too fast.'

Van Gogh painted for just ten years. But during this time he did more than 800 paintings in oil colours and 700 drawings. Surprisingly, he sold only one painting while he lived. People did not understand the way he painted. His work was too unusual and alive with energy.

Now the whole world knows he was a great artist.

LEARN MORE! READ THESE ARTICLES...
THE NETHERLANDS (VOLUME 6) • PAINTING (VOLUME 3) • SUNFLOWERS (VOLUME 10)

SEARCH LIGHT

How many paintings did van Gogh sell in his lifetime?
a) 80
b) 700
c) 1

Van Gogh's paintings of sunflowers are probably some of the most famous paintings in the world. You may even have seen them on T-shirts and coffee mugs. This is a photo of an original, painted in 1889.
© Christie's Images/Corbis

Answer: c) 1

Lonely Landscapes

Xia Gui is known today as one of China's greatest masters of **landscape** painting. He painted rapidly, using short, sharp strokes of the brush. Most of his landscapes were done in shades of black, but a few had light washes of colour added to them.

Xia was probably the official court painter to either the emperor Ningzong or the emperor Lizong (or maybe both). That means he would have lived about the end of the 12th century to the beginning of the 13th century.

Together with his friend and fellow artist Ma Yuan, Xia founded the Ma-Xia school of painting. This group followed a tradition of very simple landscape painting, with little happening in the landscape and few details. By showing only selected features, such as mountain peaks and twisted trees, they aimed to create a feeling of unlimited space and quiet drama. The Ma-Xia school had a great influence on later artists.

Most of Xia's surviving works are album leaves. These were single sheets of usually square paper, occasionally glued onto fans. The paintings were done on silk, mainly in shades of black ink. In each landscape there are distant hills in the upper left corner and a closer view of land in the lower right corner. In the centre, groups of trees reach into the empty space all around. The empty space was always an important feature of Xia's work.

Xia was also a master at **composing** works on the hand scroll. These are viewed by unrolling the scroll from one end to the other, then rerolling the scroll as you view it. The effect is like a continuous imaginary journey through the scenery of nature.

LEARN MORE! READ THESE ARTICLES...
CHINA (VOLUME 7) • EMPRESS OF PEKING (VOLUME 4)
PAINTING (VOLUME 3)

SEARCH LIGHT

Fill in the gaps:
Xia Gui made his paintings on album leaves and

_____ _____.

The painting here, known as 'Swinging Gibbon', is said to be by Xia Gui. The next generation of painters did not value Xia's work. But about 50 years after that, one critic wrote: 'His works have an exciting [stimulating] quality,...a remarkable achievement.'

DID YOU KNOW?
Rap and hip-hop grew out of the 'street music' of major urban areas, making it a modern folk music tradition.

Music of Everyday Life

Have you played or sung 'London Bridge Is Falling Down', 'Ring a Ring O'Roses', or 'Frère Jacques'? If you have, then you're part of the folk music tradition. In the case of nursery rhymes and musical games, that tradition can date back for hundreds of years!

Folk music is the shared music of a group or community of people. It's everyday music that was often created as part of children's games or as a way to make work easier. Some songs were sung at parties or weddings. Some were used to celebrate births or **mourn** deaths. And some were used as part of religious services.

Pete Seeger, musician of the folk movement of the 1950s and '60s.
© Neal Preston/Corbis

Folk music is learned and passed on by everyone, not just musicians. Many folk performers don't study music in school, but they learn songs by listening to others play and sing.

Because it usually isn't written down, folk music changes as it travels between people and countries. Songs are created or lost, and some change because of people's poor memories. Other songs are rewritten to match new times, situations, and ideas. In the United States, some jazz, blues, and **gospel** tunes have their roots in folk songs brought over hundreds of years ago by African slaves.

In the 1960s in North America, musicians such as Pete Seeger, Bob Dylan, and Joan Baez performed folk music accompanied by guitars. Today this type of 'folk' and 'folk rock' music remains very popular. And through it the Western folk tradition continues to excite and inspire new generations.

LEARN MORE! READ THESE ARTICLES...
FOLK ARTS AND CRAFTS (VOLUME 3) • LADYSMITH BLACK MAMBAZO (VOLUME 3)
MYTHS AND LEGENDS, FOLKTALES AND FABLES (VOLUME 5)

Folk music is passed from generation to generation at family gatherings like this one and other social occasions.
© Joseph Sohm–ChromoSohm Inc./Corbis

Music of an Era

SEARCH LIGHT

True or false? Popular music is a form of rock music.

Popular music is basically what its name says it is - music that is enjoyed by a very large number of people. But the modern term 'popular music' refers more particularly to music that's made by a musical entertainment business specifically in order to be sold.

Popular music (or 'pop' music) has roots in the music halls and **vaudeville** theatres of England and the United States. However, the modern popular music **industry** was truly launched with radio programming in the 20th century. Jazz music began to be heard widely in the 1920s. Country and western music's audience grew in the '20s as well. In the 1930s and '40s, big-band music was popular, and singers such as Frank Sinatra and Ella Fitzgerald found international fame.

(From left) Famed reggae musician Bob Marley of Jamaica; Celtic-New Age singer Enya of Ireland; and pop singer-songwriter Phil Collins of England.
(Left) © Jeff Albertson/Corbis; (centre and right) © Reuters NewMedia Inc./Corbis

In the mid-1950s, American rock and roll performers such as Elvis Presley and Chuck Berry commanded worldwide attention. By the 1960s, English bands such as the Beatles and the Rolling Stones were taking popular music in new directions. Rock strongly influenced disco, reggae, punk, rap, hip-hop, and other styles in the late 20th century.

Radio and the recording industry introduced non-Western cultures to these new forms of popular music. Traditional songs were performed in new styles, and at the same time, traditional instruments gave the new music an entirely different sound. This mixing of styles and sounds became 'world music' and 'worldbeat'.

Today worldbeat blends a wide range of sounds and **rhythms**. Shubha Mudgal combines India's folk and classical traditions with rock music. The Gipsy Kings mingle pop music with Spain's traditional flamenco. And popular music continues to evolve.

LEARN MORE! READ THESE ARTICLES...
COUNT BASIE (VOLUME 4) • JAZZ (VOLUME 3)
LADYSMITH BLACK MAMBAZO (VOLUME 3)

Popular music includes many different styles from many different places. The multiracial South African group Johnny Clegg and Savuka gave a strong European pop flavour to traditional Zulu music and added Zulu Inhlangwini dancing.
© Henry Diltz/Corbis

Answer: FALSE. Rock music is one of a number of kinds of popular music.

33

Who were the people most responsible for creating jazz?

Dixieland is a jazz style that grew up in New Orleans, Louisiana. Groups such as the Preservation Hall Jazz Band continue to play in this musical tradition.
© Robert Holmes/Corbis

DID YOU KNOW?

'Cool', 'bad', 'fly', 'the bomb' (later 'da bomb'), and 'dj' are all slang words that came from jazz.

The Music of Change

Jazz music is very hard to define because it changes all the time. It has its roots in America's folk traditions, especially in the music of slaves taken from Africa. But today musicians from many countries play jazz and make their own contributions to it.

Jazz funeral in New Orleans, Louisiana.
© Philip Gould/Corbis

Early jazz borrowed from slaves' field hollers (a kind of musical calling-out) and work songs and from African American **hymns** and spirituals. Soon it adopted music from funeral processions and popular dance music.

The first jazz recording was made in 1917 by the Original Dixieland Jazz Band. Dixieland grew up in New Orleans, Louisiana, and has a big brassy sound. It features trumpets, saxophones, trombones, and other wind instruments.

Chicago and New York City emerged as major jazz centres. Talented musicians such as Bix Beiderbecke and Louis Armstrong formed bands. And jazz spread to Europe. France especially welcomed jazz music and musicians - many not valued in the United States simply because they were black.

Jazz has also been richly influenced by women, especially as singers. Billie Holiday, Sarah Vaughan, and Ella Fitzgerald are just a few of the classics.

In the 1930s and '40s, jazz focused on **rhythm**, melody, and a smoother sound. Glenn Miller, Benny Goodman, Duke Ellington, and Count Basie earned fame for their 'big band' jazz orchestra styles.

In the mid-20th century, jazz changed again as mood, feeling, and complex musical imaginings dominated. Miles Davis, Charlie Parker, and John Coltrane led this 'cool' style of jazz. Davis later helped introduce 'jazz **fusion**', blending rock and other popular music with his jazz.

Jazz today is more varied than ever before. And jazz keeps growing in many directions.

LEARN MORE! READ THESE ARTICLES...
LOUIS ARMSTRONG (VOLUME 3) • COUNT BASIE (VOLUME 4)
POPULAR MUSIC (VOLUME 3)

Answer: Jazz began with the songs, chants, and music of African slaves in America.

A Very Formal Music

In the West (Europe and the Americas) the term 'classical music' usually refers to sonatas, chamber music, operas, and symphonies from the late 1700s through the 1800s.

Classical music is a very **formal** kind of music. This makes classical different from forms such as jazz or folk music. Classical music has set fairly complex patterns that all classical composers (writers of music) and musicians understand and follow.

A sonata is made up of three parts that focus, in different ways, on a main musical theme, or special tune. The first part presents the theme. In the second part the theme is developed and played in different ways. The third part repeats the theme.

A symphony is a longer **composition** created to be played by an **orchestra**. A symphony has several sections called 'movements'. One movement is usually in the form of a sonata.

SEARCH LIGHT

Fill in the gap: A symphony is a long piece of music played by an _____.

String quartet playing chamber music.
© Charles O'Rear/Corbis

Chamber music was originally created for a smaller private audience. This kind of music uses fewer musicians and features delicate musical patterns.

An opera is basically a play acted to music. The **dialogue** is sung, not spoken, and is accompanied by an orchestra.

The music of the great classical composers is still popular today. You may know the names or music of such composers as Beethoven, Mozart, and Bach.

Non-Western cultures have different forms of classical music. In China, classical music refers to ancient music that existed before the influence of Western art forms. India's two forms of classical music, Hindustani music and Karnatic music, are hundreds of years old. In Central Asia classical music comes from the medieval court music of such centres as Bukhara and Samarkand, two cities in Uzbekistan.

LEARN MORE! READ THESE ARTICLES...
LUDWIG VAN BEETHOVEN (VOLUME 3) • RAVI SHANKAR (VOLUME 3)
VIENNA (VOLUME 6)

© Kevin Fleming/Corbis

Answer: A symphony is a long piece of music played by an orchestra.

Louis Armstrong (centre) also performed in a number of films. This picture is from *High Society,* a 1956 film starring the singer Bing Crosby (seated, far left), Frank Sinatra, and Grace Kelly.
The Kobal Collection/MGM

SEARCH LIGHT

What is unusual about scat? (Hint: Bee dee wa scabba doo.)

Satchmo - Jazz Superstar

In the early 20th century, a young African American boy sang and danced on a street in New Orleans, Louisiana. He wanted to earn some money because his family was very poor. That boy, Louis Daniel Armstrong, would become one of the world's most famous jazz trumpet players.

Armstrong loved music and tried various instruments before finally choosing the cornet. The cornet looks like a trumpet but is shaped like a

Armstrong warming up on his trumpet in 1956.
© Ted Streshinsky/Corbis

cone. Armstrong became the leader of his school band. Jazz was just becoming popular, and as a teenager he learned music by listening to pieces played by famous jazz musicians. Later he learned to read music.

Armstrong played with jazz bands in Chicago and New York City. He recorded his first solo pieces, 'Chimes Blues' and 'Tears', in Chicago. In New York he changed from the cornet to the trumpet. He thought the trumpet had a brighter sound and a more flamboyant look. By the time Armstrong was 28 years old he had become very famous. He toured the world as a trumpet soloist with big bands.

Louis Armstrong was nicknamed 'Satchmo' by his fellow musicians. Short for 'Satchel Mouth', the name suggested that his mouth was as wide as a satchel (a large school bag). But the friendly teasing was a sign of the great respect jazz musicians had for Armstrong's talent. His creativity, ability to express emotion, and superior **technical** skill were universally admired.

Armstrong is also remembered as one of the inventors of what is called 'scat'. Sometimes, while singing a **lyric**, he would sing without using words. He would sing a string of sounds instead. His scat singing and gravelly voice became as well known as his face and trumpet.

LEARN MORE! READ THESE ARTICLES...
COUNT BASIE (VOLUME 4) • JAZZ (VOLUME 3) • CARLOS SANTANA (VOLUME 3)

Living for Music

Can you imagine composing music without being able to hear it? Beethoven, one of the greatest music composers ever born, created much of his best music late in life, after he had become totally deaf.

Ludwig van Beethoven was born in 1770 in Bonn, Germany. Music was very important in his family. His grandfather and his father were professional singers in the choir of the **archbishop** in Bonn. Young Beethoven was given the opportunity to play the organ at court as soon as he was old enough to work. The archbishop

Beethoven's own handwritten music for his *Eroica* symphony.
Mansell/Timepix

liked his music so much that he sent him to Vienna to learn from Wolfgang Amadeus Mozart. After hearing Beethoven play, Mozart told his friends: 'This young man will make a great name for himself in the world.'

At that time people usually thought of the piano as an instrument for playing music for singers. But Beethoven composed such beautiful piano music that it stood on its own as a work of art. Beethoven's music was a bridge between a strict musical tradition and a freer, more deeply emotional style of music. He also brought new ideas and life to such classical music forms as the sonata, symphony, concerto, and quartet. Some of his best-known works include the *Moonlight Sonata*, the *Pastoral* and *Eroica* symphonies, and the *Emperor Concerto*.

After some years Beethoven realized that he couldn't hear things clearly any more - not even what he was playing. Doctors told him he would never be cured. Beethoven stopped playing in public and kept away from people. But he still heard music in his mind and he wrote down his musical ideas in his notebooks. These books contained some of his finest music.

LEARN MORE! READ THESE ARTICLES...
CLASSICAL MUSIC (VOLUME 3) • SIGHT AND SOUND (VOLUME 2) • VIENNA (VOLUME 6)

DID YOU KNOW?
Beethoven's musical works marked the beginnings of Romantic music. That sounds like music about love. But 'romantic' more broadly describes art that is concerned with expressing emotions, dramatic things in life, and the individual person's experience.

Here, Nusrat Fateh Ali Khan and Party perform in a 1993 concert. The term 'party' is a general term for the group of musicians who play for the *qawwal*.

© BALDEV/Corbis Sygma

DID YOU KNOW?
Sufism is the Islamic belief and practice from which *qawwali* music arises. Sufi Muslims seek to find the truth about divine love and understanding through direct personal experience of God.

Centre Stage of Qawwali

Nusrat Fateh Ali Khan was considered one of the greatest singers of the music known as *qawwali*. Begun in Persia (present-day Iran) hundreds of years ago, *qawwali* music is based on Sufi Muslim poems about deep religious faith expressed through love. It has simple melodies and forceful rhythms.

*Qawwal*s (singers of *qawwali*) traditionally perform their songs at **shrines**. A *qawwal* must learn all the Sufi poems. He often makes up more

Nusrat Fateh Ali Khan in concert.
Michael Harder Photography

*qawwali*s by using phrases and passages from different poems to create a new expression or idea. The singing includes much shouting and dancing.

Nusrat Fateh Ali Khan was born in 1948 in Pakistan. His father and two of his uncles were also famous *qawwal*s who sang in the classical style. Khan received music lessons from his father. When his father died in 1964, Khan sang in the *qawwali* style for the first time at his father's funeral. Two years later Khan gave his first public performance, singing with his uncles.

Khan sang in a very high range (a family trademark) and had a powerfully expressive voice. He was noted for his melodic creativity and had been known to perform for 10 hours. By the early 1970s Khan was recognized throughout Pakistan as the outstanding *qawwal* of his time. He sang at a world music concert in the United Kingdom in 1985. Soon he was performing regularly throughout Europe.

In 1996 Khan recorded songs for several American films. He also appeared on music television shows and performed songs that appealed specifically to Western audiences. Some people felt that he had betrayed the music's Islamic heritage. But Khan said he had given up nothing to share his musical heritage with a wider audience.

LEARN MORE! READ THESE ARTICLES…
FOLK MUSIC (VOLUME 3) • ISLAM (VOLUME 5)
PAKISTAN: A YOUNG COUNTRY WITH AN ANCIENT
HISTORY (VOLUME 7)

SEARCH LIGHT

Fill in the gaps: *Qawwali* music is based on

_____ _____.

The South African Sound

In the past 20 years, the music of South Africa has spread all over the world. In part that's thanks to Ladysmith Black Mambazo, the country's most popular singing group. But to find out what Ladysmith is and what 'mambazo' means, we have to go back to South African mining towns in the 1960s.

Working in the mines kept black workers far from their homes and their families. So on Saturday nights they entertained themselves by holding singing contests featuring traditional Zulu harmonies.

That was how a young man named Joseph Shabalala discovered his singing talent. In 1964, Shabalala kept having a dream in which he heard a special harmony. To create that sound, he formed a music group with his brothers, Headman and Jockey, and some cousins and friends.

They called themselves Ladysmith Black Mambazo because Ladysmith is Shabalala's hometown, and the black ox is the strongest animal on a farm. The group 'chopped down' their competition in every singing contest, so they added the name Mambazo, which is a kind of ax.

Years later American musician Paul Simon heard the group's singing and later met the members in South Africa. They performed on Simon's 1986 album *Graceland* and toured with him, sharing their music with people everywhere. A year later Ladysmith Black Mambazo won a Grammy - an American music award - and today they're Africa's top-selling music group.

Shabalala also keeps the folk music of South Africa alive by teaching the traditional songs to young children.

DID YOU KNOW?
Ladysmith Black Mambazo has recorded songs for many films, including *The Lion King II*, and has performed for both the pope and the queen of England.

SEARCH LIGHT

What does 'Mambazo' mean in the name Ladysmith Black Mambazo?

LEARN MORE! READ THESE ARTICLES...
FOLK MUSIC (VOLUME 3) • POPULAR MUSIC (VOLUME 3)
SOUTH AFRICA (VOLUME 8)

Answer: Mambazo is a type of ax, used in the name because the group 'cut down' their singing competitors.

Rock Guitarist

Carlos Santana was born in Mexico in 1947. He came by his interest in music naturally, since his father played violin in a traditional Mexican mariachi band. At about 7 years old, Carlos began to study guitar. He tried to copy the music of famous guitarists he heard on the radio.

As time passed, Carlos grew more interested in rock music and the blues. He began playing in bands as a teenager, and even after his family moved to California, he returned to Mexico to play in clubs and bars. In San Francisco in 1966, Carlos founded a group with five other musicians. The group's name, the Santana Blues Band, was later shortened to Santana.

In three years the group shot to fame when it performed at the historic 1969 Woodstock rock festival in the United States. The band became known for mixing jazz and Latin music into a rock sound. Carlos' own playing featured a unique, exciting electric guitar sound. His long and complex guitar solos varied and developed a single musical **theme**.

The group's first three albums were all major hits. The music was **vivid** and sparked the audience's imagination. On later albums the band continued to experiment with mixing jazz and rock.

In 1998 the group was named to the Rock and Roll Hall of Fame. The following year Carlos Santana released *Supernatural*. On this CD he performed songs with such top performers as Eric Clapton, Lauryn Hill, Dave Matthews, and Rob Thomas of Matchbox 20. The CD sold more than 20 million copies, Santana's greatest success ever. And it introduced a new generation of listeners to him.

SEARCH LIGHT

Which three styles of music has Carlos Santana combined in his own work?

DID YOU KNOW?

Carlos Santana's hit album *Supernatural* reflected the continuing influence of Latin music in his own. Many songs on that CD, as on his earlier recordings, were sung in Spanish.

LEARN MORE! READ THESE ARTICLES...
COUNT BASIE (VOLUME 4)
POPULAR MUSIC (VOLUME 3)
RAVI SHANKAR (VOLUME 3)

Answer: Santana's music combines jazz, Latin music, and rock.

Music at His Fingertips

SEARCH LIGHT

Which instrument did Ravi Shankar play and make famous?
a) sitar
b) drums
c) cymbals

In 1930, at age 10, Ravi Shankar and other family members joined his eldest brother's Indian dance **troupe** in Paris, France. The boy lived in France for over five years and studied dance and music.

Shankar gave up dance at age 18. He returned to India and studied the sitar for seven years under master musician Ustad Allauddin Khan. The sitar is a large long-necked stringed instrument, played from a seated position.

In 1944 Shankar began composing film music. A bit later he became music director of All India Radio. His audience grew within India. And when his musical **score** for Satyajit Ray's 1955 film *Pather Panchali* won major awards, Shankar gained worldwide notice.

Shankar first toured the United States and England in 1956. Over the next ten years his audiences grew from small groups of Indian immigrants to sold-out concerts at New York City's Philharmonic Hall. As Shankar's fame increased, so did the popularity of Indian music. Sitar music is very different from music of the West. So it was exciting for Shankar and others to combine the two traditions to make altogether new sounds.

Ravi Shankar and daughter Anoushka performing at a charity concert in Kuala Lumpur, Malaysia, in 2001.
© AFP/Corbis

Shankar met and worked with many famous Western musicians who played a variety of styles. He played with jazz musicians, classical violinist Yehudi Menuhin, pianist and **conductor** André Previn, and experimental composer Philip Glass. His most famous musical association was with rock musician George Harrison of the Beatles. Harrison studied sitar under Shankar in India. Harrison's fame and influence allowed him to introduce Shankar and Indian music to a vast audience in the West.

Shankar continues to compose and perform. And he remains one of the most highly regarded musicians in the world.

LEARN MORE! READ THESE ARTICLES...
INDIA (VOLUME 7) • POPULAR MUSIC (VOLUME 3) • SATYAJIT RAY (VOLUME 3)

In 1971 George Harrison organized the Concert for Bangladesh.
Ravi Shankar and many other musicians performed to raise money
for the starving people of that country.
© Henry Diltz/Corbis

DID YOU KNOW?

The most frequently played South Asian musical form for sitar is called a *raga*. The sitarist, accompanied by *tabla* (drum) and *tamboura* (droning lute), plays a particular set of notes in a very specific way to create a unique mood.

Writing for the Ages

Literature is writing that is good enough or important enough to last for tens, hundreds, or even thousands of years. It's valuable work that people make sure is heard, read, and passed down from generation to generation.

People usually think of literature as novels such as *Kidnapped*, the poetry of Emily Dickinson, or the plays of William Shakespeare. But even

© Royalty-Free/Corbis

books for young readers, such as *The Cat in the Hat* or *Alice's Adventures in Wonderland*, can be literature. Literature also includes philosophy and history, letters and essays, even journals like *The Diary of Anne Frank*. Some literature tells a story; some literature makes a point; and some literature just uses words and language in an exciting or memorable way. Some literature does all these things at once.

Not all literature started on the page. Ancient stories of heroes like Beowulf and Odysseus were spoken first and written down later. Speeches such as Martin Luther King, Jr.'s *I Have a Dream* can also be literature.

But just writing something down doesn't make it literature. We don't usually think of such useful but disposable things as phone books, menus, or game instructions as literature. Even books come and go - many that you see in shops today won't be around decades from now. Most newspaper articles are read once and tossed aside, but if their topics are important or their writing is very good, those articles might be collected into a book to be preserved and reread. They're on their way to becoming literature!

LEARN MORE! READ THESE ARTICLES...
ISABEL ALLENDE (VOLUME 4)
RABINDRANATH TAGORE (VOLUME 3)
JULES VERNE (VOLUME 3)

DID YOU KNOW?

Literature depends on the taste of the time. When it was given in 1863, Lincoln's Gettysburg Address was considered poorly written. Today people have forgotten the other speech given that day, and Lincoln's speech is thought of as great literature.

SEARCH LIGHT

Which of the following would have the best chance of someday being considered literature?
a) phone book
b) restaurant menu
c) your diary
d) CD-ROM instructions

Answer: c) your diary

Haiku Master

The poet Basho was born Matsuo Munefusa in 1644. He is considered to be the greatest of the Japanese *haiku* poets. Basho took his name from the Japanese term *basho-an*, meaning 'cottage of the plantain tree' (a plantain is like a banana). This was a simple place where the poet liked to go to be by himself.

Haiku is a traditional form of Japanese poetry that puts great emotion in just a few words. *Haiku* poems have only three lines and a total of only 17 syllables. And they are often about nature.

Although he was interested in poetry from a young age, Matsuo wasn't always a poet. He started out as a **samurai** warrior in the service of a local lord. But after his lord's death in 1666, Matsuo gave up being a warrior and focused on creating poetry. He moved to Japan's capital, Tokyo (at that time called Edo), and soon became well known as a poet and **critic**.

Basho brought a new style of *haiku* to Japanese poetry. In the past, it had basically been a hobby and not very serious, but Basho brought his Buddhist beliefs to his writing. He looked with interest at small things and showed the connections between all things. His new-style *haiku* compared two separate physical events. In the following *haiku*, for example, he links nightfall with the landing of a black crow.

On a withered branch
A crow has alighted:
Nightfall in autumn.

(Note: Unlike the original, this **translation** has only 16 syllables.)

Basho wrote poems as he traveled around the islands of Japan. He wrote about the sights and landscapes he saw, and these poems are considered some of his best.

LEARN MORE! READ THESE ARTICLES…
BUDDHISM (VOLUME 5) • HIROSHIGE (VOLUME 3)
JAPAN: MODERN NATION OF ANCIENT TRADITIONS (VOLUME 7)

DID YOU KNOW?
A term often used to describe Basho's poetry is *sabi*. The word refers to a love of the old, the faded, and the little-noticed.

SEARCH LIGHT

Basho's name came from his
a) cottage.
b) village.
c) lord.

Answer: a) cottage.

Uruguayan President Jorge Batlle (left) and Argentine
Chancellor Adalberto Rodríguez Giavariani admire a
portrait of Jorge Luis Borges painted by Jorge Demirjian.

DID YOU KNOW?

Borges is reported
to have once said,
'Not granting me
the Nobel Prize
has become a
Scandinavian
tradition; since I
was born they have
not been granting
it to me.'

Creator of Fantastical Fictions

Can you imagine a garden where a beautiful poppy flower has the power to unravel time? Or a pool where if you gaze too long into it, you could merge with your reflection? Jorge Luis Borges imagined these things and more as he created **fantastical** worlds with his words.

Borges was born in 1899, in Buenos Aires, Argentina. His father was a lawyer and his mother was a teacher. His English-born

Borges on his 82nd birthday, in 1981.
© Bettmann/Corbis

grandmother told him many stories. Borges was educated at home by an English governess and learned English before Spanish.

At age 20 Borges started writing poems, essays, and a biography. But when his father died in 1938, Borges had to take up a job as a librarian to support the family. The same year, Borges suffered a severe head wound that left him near death, unable to speak, and afraid he was insane. This experience seems to have freed in him a great creativity. When he finished his library work, he would spend the rest of the day reading and writing.

Borges' dreamlike short stories would later make him famous when they were collected in the books *Ficciones* (*Fictions*) and *The Aleph and Other Stories, 1933-69*. He also wrote political articles that angered the Argentine government and cost him his library job.

In 1956 Borges received Argentina's national prize for literature. But he had been losing his eyesight for decades because of a rare disease and by this time he was completely blind. Still, he created stories by having his mother and friends write as he **dictated**. Some of his best work was produced this way, including *El libro de los seres imaginarios* (*The Book of Imaginary Beings*).

LEARN MORE! READ THESE ARTICLES...
ISABEL ALLENDE (VOLUME 4) • ARGENTINA (VOLUME 9) • LITERATURE (VOLUME 3)

Although Borges is famous as a Spanish-language writer, what language did he learn first?

Answer: Because his governess was English, Borges learned English before Spanish.

Prized Poet
of Illinois

Gwendolyn Brooks was born in 1917 and grew up in Chicago, Illinois, U.S. That city would play a major part in the life and work of this important American poet. She began writing poetry when she was just 7 years old. By the time she was in her early teens, her writing was being published in magazines.

Brooks, an African American, attended what was then the leading secondary school for white children in Chicago. This was very unusual at the time. She was later transferred to an all-black school and then to an **integrated** school. These experiences gave her an insight into the relationships between black people and white people that strongly influenced her work.

Gwendolyn Brooks was the first African American poet to
a) win the Nobel Prize.
b) be published in the United States.
c) win the Pulitzer Prize.

Gwendolyn Brooks with her first published book, *A Street in Bronzeville* (1945).

AP/Wide World Photos

Brooks's first published book, *A Street in Bronzeville* (1945), won rave reviews. Its poems made the ordinary life of her neighbours seem special to the reader. In 1950, Brooks won the Pulitzer Prize for Poetry with *Annie Allen*. She was the first African American poet to win this award. The book's poems focus on an African American girl growing up in Chicago.

In the late 1960s, Brooks's poetry became more **political**. She began to think that 'black poets should write as blacks, about blacks, and address themselves to blacks.' In 1968 she published *In the Mecca*. The book's long title poem reflects the pain and struggle of African American people living in the Mecca, a vast block of flats that had become part of a **slum**.

Brooks wrote many more books. She was honoured as **poet laureate** of Illinois (1968) and held a similar position for the whole United States (1985-86). Throughout her life Brooks remained strongly committed to teaching about the power of poetry and to encouraging young writers.

LEARN MORE! READ THESE ARTICLES...
MARTIN LUTHER KING, JR. (VOLUME 4) • LITERATURE (VOLUME 3)
UNITED STATES: A YOUNG AND POWERFUL NATION (VOLUME 9)

DID YOU KNOW?

Gwendolyn Brooks, who helped so many young poets herself, was helped by others when she was young. The African American poets James Weldon Johnson and Langston Hughes personally urged her to read and write poetry.

Answer: c) win the Pulitzer Prize.

SEARCH LIGHT

Fill in
the gaps:
In addition to
being an author,
Lewis Carroll
was a

_____
_____.

Lewis Carroll's characters from *Alice's Adventures in Wonderland* are still some of the most popular in the world.
© Craig Lovell/Corbis

DID YOU KNOW?
Dodgson invented the name Lewis Carroll by taking his first and middle names, Charles Lutwidge, and translating them into Latin as *Carolus Ludovicus*. Then he reversed them and translated the Latin back into English.

The Man Who Created Wonderland

Not many people curl up in their favourite chair to read a maths book. But in the 1800s, a maths lecturer named Charles Dodgson wrote two children's books that are still popular today. Using the pen name 'Lewis

Lewis Carroll (Charles Dodgson).
© Bettmann/Corbis

Carroll', Dodgson dreamed up *Alice's Adventures in Wonderland* and its sequel, *Through the Looking-Glass*.

As a boy growing up in the English countryside, Lewis Carroll (as we'll refer to Dodgson) loved mathematical puzzles. As an adult, that love led him to teach maths at the University of Oxford.

Carroll never married, but he loved entertaining children. He was especially fond of the daughters of the **dean** of his college - Alice, Lorina, and Edith Liddell. Carroll often took the girls on boating and picnic trips and amused them by making up stories and drawing pictures. One story told of a young girl named Alice who fell down a rabbit hole into Wonderland, a magical place where nothing was as it seemed.

Young Alice Liddell asked Carroll to write the story down. He did, filling it with his imagination and humour and also with his knack for puzzles and word games. It became *Alice's Adventures in Wonderland*, a wild tale that includes an anxious White Rabbit, a vanishing Cheshire Cat, and a tea party thrown by a Mad Hatter.

Carroll had not intended to publish the story as a book, but his friends talked him into it. Readers loved the strange and silly adventures, and so Carroll continued Alice's tale in *Through the Looking-Glass*. By the time he died, Carroll's two Alice books were the most popular children's books in England.

LEARN MORE! READ THESE ARTICLES…
CHARLES DICKENS (VOLUME 3) • LITERATURE (VOLUME 3)
JULES VERNE (VOLUME 4)

Answer: In addition to being an author, Lewis Carroll was a maths lecturer.

59

A Life of Letters and Literature

Emily Dickinson, one of America's greatest poets, was born in 1830 in Massachusetts, U.S. She had many friends, though she did not often leave her home to meet them. After 1865 she seldom left her room, appearing only occasionally and briefly in a white dress when guests visited downstairs.

Dickinson spent a great deal of time writing to her friends. The greatest excitement in Dickinson's life was in her **vivid** imagination. She included many of her best poems in the letters she wrote. She also wrote or copied poems into little booklets that she made by sewing pages together.

For the time in which she lived, Dickinson's poems were unusual. Most of them are about familiar things such as love and friendship, nature and death. But her rhymes are often not quite exact, and some of her poems are like a puzzle. But many people find great beauty and truth in her words.

Her poems are especially remarkable because of the strong effect they have, even though they're usually very brief. She stripped away unnecessary words and made sure that those that remained were **energetic** and exact. She also liked to place a familiar word in an unusual position to 'surprise' us and to make us pay attention.

Many people think that the poems of Emily Dickinson are among the best ever written by an American poet. It seems strange, then, that only seven of her poems were published while she was alive. It was Dickinson's sister, Lavinia, who first published her poems in a book. She called it *Poems by Emily Dickinson*. It was published in 1890, four years after Emily died.

LEARN MORE! READ THESE ARTICLES...
BASHO (VOLUME 3) • LITERATURE (VOLUME 3)
NORTH AMERICA (VOLUME 9)

SEARCH LIGHT

Fill in the gap: Dickinson often sent her poems in _____ to her friends.

DID YOU KNOW?

Here is a sample of Dickinson's poetry:

The bee is not afraid of me,
I know the butterfly;
The pretty people in the woods
Receive me cordially.

The brooks laugh louder when I come,
The breezes madder play.
Wherefore, mine eyes, thy silver mists?
Wherefore, O summer's day?

Answer: Dickinson often sent her poems in letters to her friends.

The Nobel Laureate

When Wole Soyinka was a child, his grandfather told him how to deal with a bully. 'Even if you are beaten, challenge him again. I promise you, either you will defeat him or he will run away.'

These words turned out to be true for Wole Soyinka, the first black African writer to win the Nobel Prize for Literature. The bully he fought - with his words, not his fists - was the Nigerian military government. Even when the government put him into prison, he continued to write his stories, novels, essays, poetry, and plays.

Soyinka was born in 1934 in Nigeria. His full name is Akinwande Oluwole Soyinka. His large family is of Yoruba heritage. And having a big family, he got to listen to lots of stories - about battles, religion, legends, and family.

Soyinka attended university in England but returned to Nigeria to study African drama. He also taught drama and literature at Nigerian universities.

Wole Soyinka in 1986.
© Jacques Langevin/Corbis

In 1960 he founded a theatre group, where he put on his own plays and even acted in some. His first important play, *A Dance of the Forests*, was about Nigerian independence. In *The Lion and the Jewel*, Soyinka made fun of Westernized African school teachers.

During the Nigerian **civil war**, Soyinka worked for a cease-fire and was arrested because of his work and writings. The government placed him in a cell all by himself for over a year. Only his own ideas kept him entertained. These ideas became some of his later books.

Soyinka's plays draw on Nigerian culture, dance, poetry, music, and myths. These elements combine with his wide knowledge and his strong political beliefs to create powerful dramatic images and ideas.

LEARN MORE! READ THESE ARTICLES...
NIGERIA (VOLUME 8) • A NIGERIAN FOLKTALE: THE MONKEY COURT (VOLUME 5)
THEATRE (VOLUME 3)

SEARCH LIGHT

Fill in the gap: Soyinka was imprisoned for disagreeing with the Nigerian _____.

Soyinka's plays have been staged worldwide. *Death and the King's Horseman* (shown here at the Goodman Theatre in Chicago, Illinois, U.S.) dramatizes the conflict between Western morals and African culture and traditions.
The Goodman Theatre; photo by James C. Clark

DID YOU KNOW?
Soyinka often refers to the Yoruba god Ogun as an important figure for him, his writing, and his people. He describes Ogun as 'the god of creativity and destruction'. Ogun is traditionally the god of war, the hunt, and ironworking.

Answer: Soyinka was imprisoned for disagreeing with the Nigerian government.

63

Rabindranath Tagore, seen here with his granddaughter in 1929, is generally considered the most outstanding artist of modern India.

SEARCH LIGHT

Rabindranath Tagore is famous as the first Indian to do what?

Poet Laureate
of India

Rabindranath Tagore, born in 1861 in Calcutta, India, started writing poems when he was only 8 years old. He grew up to be the first Indian writer to receive the Nobel Prize for Literature.

Tagore studied in India and London, England. In 1890 he published *Manasi*, his first collection of truly fine poems. In 1891 he went to East Bengal (now Bangladesh) to help manage his family's lands. He found the village people kind but very poor. Tagore wrote many poems and stories about their condition. He also wrote about the beautiful Bengali countryside, especially the Padma River.

Tagore wrote in new forms of verse and in the common language of the Bengali people, rather than in **classical** styles. His writings became very popular amongst all Bengalis. His poems of 1901-07 reflect his great sadness at the death of his wife and two of his children. In 1910 he wrote a little book of devotional songs called *Gitanjali*. It was translated into many languages and became a huge success. In 1913 he won the Nobel Prize for Literature.

Tagore produced 22 collections of writings during his life. He wrote songs, plays, short stories, and books, and he composed music. He also founded a school in rural West Bengal that combined European and Indian traditions. It later became Vishva-Bharati University.

In 1915 the British government knighted Tagore. Four years later he gave up his knighthood after a terrible shooting of Indians by British soldiers. All his life he spoke out against British rule of India.

Tagore lectured and read his works to people in many countries from about 1912. And at about age 70 he took up painting and became one of India's finest artists.

LEARN MORE! READ THESE ARTICLES...
BANGLADESH (VOLUME 7) • LITERATURE (VOLUME 3)
RAVI SHANKAR (VOLUME 3)

DID YOU KNOW?

Rabindranath Tagore's father was a major Hindu thinker. He founded a quiet getaway in rural West Bengal (a state of India), where his son set up his experimental school.

Answer: Tagore is famous for being the first Indian to win the Nobel Prize for Literature.

Journey to Everywhere

SEARCH LIGHT

How did studying geography and science help Verne's writing? (Hint: He liked to write about things that might happen.)

Imagine exploring a distant land in a giant balloon. You could drift over mountains and waterfalls, deep blue lakes, and flaming volcanoes.

Jules Verne.
© Rykoff Collection/Corbis

A French writer named Jules Verne imagined such a journey many years ago. He wrote about it in a book called *Five Weeks in a Balloon* (1863). It was his first adventure story about strange journeys. People liked the story so much that Verne decided to write more. The next one was called *A Journey to the Centre of the Earth* (1864). It was about all the wonderful and scary things people might find inside the Earth.

As a young boy Verne often went sailing with his brother on the River Loire in France. Verne would imagine that he was sailing a huge **yacht** on a voyage of discovery. Verne wrote about his imaginary adventures in the sea in *Twenty Thousand Leagues Under the Sea* (1870). He named his imaginary submarine the *Nautilus*, after an actual submarine built in 1800. In *From the Earth to the Moon* (1865) he wrote about travelling to the Moon in a rocketship long before powered flight was even possible.

People have said that Verne invented the future. It would be more accurate to say that he invented **science fiction**. Verne himself said that he was fortunate to live and write in a time when new discoveries and inventions were being made. He kept up with advances in geography and science to get ideas for his stories. Verne believed the discoveries he studied would someday make his imaginary journeys a reality.

LEARN MORE! READ THESE ARTICLES...
ASTRONAUTS (VOLUME 2) • LEWIS CARROLL (VOLUME 3)
SUBMARINES (VOLUME 2)

Like many of Jules Verne's novels, *Twenty Thousand Leagues Under the Sea* is filled with fantastical creatures and exciting places.
© Bettmann/Corbis

DID YOU KNOW?
Not long after the success of Verne's book *Around the World in 80 Days* (1873), journalist Nellie Bly attempted the around-the-world journey. She finished in 72 days.

Answer: Studying geography helped Verne set his fantasy stories in realistic places to make them seem more real. His knowledge of science helped his invented machines seem more possible.

SEARCH LIGHT

Find and correct the mistake in the following sentence: Walker was the first Aboriginal woman to be noticed.

As a young woman, Kath Walker was angry about how Aboriginal people were treated. She then began working to have the laws made more fair - and she succeeded in many ways.

Aboriginal Poet

She was born Kathleen Jean Mary Ruska, but she's known in the Aboriginal language as Oodgeroo Noonuccal. Her Aboriginal last name,

Kath Walker (Aboriginal name Oodgeroo Noonuccal) as an older woman.
National Archives of Australia/Canberra, Act, Australia

Noonuccal, is the name of her clan. Kath Walker, the name she wrote under for most of her career, became a famous Australian Aboriginal writer and political protester. In fact, when her book of poetry, *We Are Going,* came out in 1964, she became the first Aboriginal woman to be published.

Walker grew up in Queensland, Australia, where many of the ancient Aboriginal customs were still practiced. At the time Walker was growing up, Aboriginal people had few rights in Australia. She was allowed to go to school only through the primary grades.

When she was 13, Walker began work as a maid. At 16 she wanted to become a nurse but wasn't allowed to because she was Aboriginal. What Walker did instead was work hard for Aboriginal rights. In 1967 she was successful in getting the anti-Aboriginal sections removed from the Australian constitution. In recognition of her efforts, she was awarded the MBE (Member of the Order of the British Empire) in 1970. Walker would later give back this award to protest further discrimination against Aboriginal people. After 1981 most of her work was published under her Aboriginal name.

Walker described her poetry as easy to understand, with simple rhymes and images. Her work focuses on the troubles of the Aboriginal people. Below is a sample of her poetry.

> But I'll tell instead of brave and fine
> when lives of black and white entwine.
> And men in brotherhood combine,
> this would I tell you, son of mine.

LEARN MORE! READ THESE ARTICLES…
AUSTRALIA (VOLUME 7) • GWENDOLYN BROOKS (VOLUME 3)
CATHY FREEMAN (VOLUME 4)

DID YOU KNOW?
Walker was left-handed, but her teachers in school forced her to write with her right hand. Not long ago, this practice was common in many places. Right-handedness was thought to be somehow 'better' and 'normal'.

Answer: Walker was the first Aboriginal woman to be published.

Moving to Rhythms

Thousands of years ago, early groups of people came together to dance. Hundreds of years ago, people danced at great functions in the courts of kings. Today, when people gather at social events, they still dance.

(Top) Balinese dancers from Indonesia. (Bottom) Gitaga drummers and dancers of Burundi.

Dancing is one of the oldest and most popular of forms of human **expression**. Originally, there were two kinds of dance. Social dances were performed on special occasions, such as births or marriages. Religious dances were performed to ask the gods for help, such as to provide rain or cure the sick.

Over the years, many early forms developed into folk dances. These continue to be enjoyed to traditional music. Some dances, however, became the specialty of professional artists. This kind of dance tends to be more theatrical and creative.

Ballet dancing developed in Europe, where it became an especially graceful art form. Ballet dancers must train constantly for years to master difficult steps, turns, and leaps. With great strength and beauty, ballet dancers can tell a story through their movements. *Swan Lake* is one such famous story ballet about a princess turned into a swan.

Twentieth-century modern dance in the West took a different approach. Often it didn't try to tell a story. Instead, the dancers worked to express pure emotions or ideas. And where ballet conveys a sense of lightness, modern dance seems much more 'earthbound'.

In Asia, different traditions arose, producing classical dance-dramas that are highly **stylized** or formal. Some Asian dances involve not only **intricate** steps but detailed hand and arm movements as well. India's classical dance has more than 4,000 *mudra*s, or gestures portraying complex actions, emotions, and relationships. In Thailand, one traditional dance is performed with lit candles.

LEARN MORE! READ THESE ARTICLES...
FANNY ELSSLER (VOLUME 4) • POPULAR MUSIC (VOLUME 3)
MARIA TALLCHIEF (VOLUME 3)

SEARCH LIGHT

Originally there were two kinds of dance, social dance and what else?

DID YOU KNOW?

Tap dance, a major feature of musical theatre, apparently developed from very mixed sources. These include the traditional clog dance of northern England, the jigs and flings of Ireland and Scotland, and the rhythmic foot stamping of African dances.

Native American girl doing a traditional dance.
© Lindsay Hebberd/Corbis

Answer: Religious dance was the other kind of dance besides social dance.

71

Life Re-created
on a Stage

Plays and drama in some form have been a part of all cultures throughout the world for all of human history. The making and overall experience of a dramatic performance is called 'theatre'.

At first, theatre was part of religious celebrations. Until several hundred years ago, most people couldn't read. Seeing the religious stories acted out helped them better understand their religions.

Actors in traditional Japanese Kabuki drama.
© Charles & Josette Lenars/Corbis

Theatre gradually developed into an art form. Plays were written and performed for entertainment and to communicate ideas. As theatre developed, so did a whole group of professional artists around it. Today the theatre employs a great many creative people doing different jobs to make and run a play.

The playwright is the person who writes the words and basic actions of a play - this is called a 'script'. The play's director reads the script and thinks of a way to turn the words and actions into a live performance. The actors learn the lines of the script and pretend to be the characters in the story.

Another important group of theatre artists are the designers. These behind-the-scenes people invent and build the environment of the play: the actors' costumes and makeup, the special lighting, any sound or music that's needed, props or properties (objects) used in the play, and the set or scenery the play is performed on. The stage set consists of the background, the furniture, and the artificial rooms that are built onstage.

All these people and elements build a fascinating dramatic world. Whether the audience is watching a Japanese Kabuki drama or a professional Shakespeare production or a school play, they partake, for a time, in the very special world of the imagination.

LEARN MORE! READ THESE ARTICLES...
SARAH BERNHARDT (VOLUME 3) • CINEMA (VOLUME 3)
WILLIAM SHAKESPEARE (VOLUME 4)

SEARCH LIGHT

Fill in the gap: The _____ decides how best to perform the story of the play.

Theatrical performances most often take place indoors. But people often enjoy outdoor stagings, especially when the weather is pleasant. This one in Toronto, Ontario, Canada, is a play by William Shakespeare.
© Bob Krust/Corbis

DID YOU KNOW?

The Mousetrap, a mystery play by Agatha Christie, has been running in London for more than 50 years - longer than any other play.

Answer: The director decides how best to perform the story of the play.

73

SEARCH LIGHT

Which musical instrument often provided music in cinemas during silent films?

DID YOU KNOW?
The amazing effect of parting the Red Sea in Cecil B. DeMille's 1923 film *The Ten Commandments* was created by using an 18-metre tub of jelly.

Dreams on the Big Screen

When Thomas A. Edison introduced a moving picture machine in 1894, only one person at a time could watch his Kinetoscope. But soon films were being projected onto a large screen for large audiences.

The earliest films were silent. Words were put up on the screen between scenes to show the **dialogues** or to help explain the action. Cinemas often used a pipe organ to provide live music.

The first feature film was *The Great Train Robbery*, a 10-minute action film made in 1903. Audiences were thrilled with this silent story of the hold-up of a moving train. Some people even fainted during the final scene when an actor turned and fired his gun at the camera.

The Kobal Collection–Kennedy Miller

© Bettmann/Corbis

The Kobal Collection–Melampo Cinematografica/Sergio Strizzi

The Kobal Collection–Biograf Jan Sverak/Portobello Pictures

(Clockwise from top) *The Great Train Robbery* (1903); Italian actor-writer-director Roberto Benigni's *La Vita è Bella* (1997; *Life Is Beautiful*); Czech director Jan Sverak's *Kolya* (1996); and Australian director John Duigan's *Flirting* (1989).

In 1927 *The Jazz Singer* marked the beginning of sound in cinema. The first 'talkies' were hard to understand. But the **technology** improved, and by 1931 very few silent pictures were still being made.

American gangster films, westerns, horror films, and musicals became very popular. Cartoons were also popular, especially those made by Walt Disney's company. Film classics from Europe include Jean Renoir's dramas and Sergei Eisenstein's war epics. In the 1950s many people began to think of some directors as the 'authors' of their films. These directors include Alfred Hitchcock, Satyajit Ray, Ingmar Bergman, and Federico Fellini.

Today India and Hong Kong have large film industries. And countries such as Iran, Mexico, Taiwan, France, Spain, and Japan produce especially beautiful, interesting films. In the late 20th century both Australia and Ireland became known for their sensitive and witty films. And, of course, America is the home of the grand and expensive **blockbuster**.

LEARN MORE! READ THESE ARTICLES...
AKIRA KUROSAWA (VOLUME 3) • MOTION PICTURES (VOLUME 2)
SATYAJIT RAY (VOLUME 3)

Director Alfred Hitchcock's *Spellbound* (1945).
© John Springer Collection/Corbis

Answer: The pipe organ often accompanied silent films.

A Grand Musical Play

SEARCH LIGHT

Find and correct the error in the following sentence: In an opera, performers usually speak their lines.

Like a play, an opera is a story acted out onstage. But in an opera the performers sing their lines instead of speaking them. An opera is also different from a musical because opera performers usually don't speak at all. Their songs don't happen between conversations, but rather their songs are the conversations. The music an orchestra plays for an opera is as important to the overall effect as the singing.

Traditional opera tells a big story in a grand way. The story is usually serious, though there are comic operas too. Many operas tell tragic tales of lovers who are kept apart. Richard Wagner's *Tristan und Isolde* is one of these. Some operas, like Wolfgang Amadeus Mozart's *The*

Outdoor performance of the opera *Aida* by Giuseppe Verdi.
© Gail Mooney/Corbis

Magic Flute, tell stories of mystery and enchantment. Comic operas, such as Gioacchino Rossini's *The Barber of Seville*, often feature silly situations and people.

In the late 1800s, W.S. Gilbert and Arthur Sullivan wrote comic operas that made fun of people from various walks of life. One of the most popular of their light operas, or operettas, was *The Pirates of Penzance*. But today's opera composers continue the dramatic spirit of classic opera, even though their subjects have changed.

A special form of opera developed in China during the late 18th century. It is called *jingxi*, and English speakers know it as Peking opera. Its performers use larger-than-life movements to **portray** their characters. The **rhythmic** beating of clappers marks time for movements, and the performance may feature acrobatic fighting scenes.

LEARN MORE! READ THESE ARTICLES...
WOLFGANG AMADEUS MOZART (VOLUME 4) • JOAN SUTHERLAND (VOLUME 4)
KIRI TE KANAWA (VOLUME 3)

Jingxi, known in English as Peking opera,
is a spectacular musical and dramatic show.
© Marc Garanger/Corbis

DID YOU KNOW?
Classic operas are usually performed in the language they were written in. Today, if the audience doesn't speak the language of the opera, the opera company may show the singers' words in the audience's language on a screen above the stage.

Enriching American Dance

Alvin Ailey was born in 1931, in Texas, U.S. As a child, he helped his mother pick cotton to earn money. They moved to Los Angeles when Ailey was about 11 years old.

In Los Angeles, Ailey discovered dance during a school field trip to a ballet performance. He began to study with the dance teacher Lester Horton and joined the Lester Horton Dance Theater in 1949. When Horton died four years later Ailey became the director of the company. However, the next year the company broke up and Ailey moved to New York City.

Alvin Ailey in 1983.
© Bettmann/Corbis

In New York Ailey danced in many performances and worked with some famous dance **choreographers**. They included Martha Graham and Hanya Holm. Ailey's own modern dancing combined what he learned from Lester Horton with African and Afro-Caribbean styles.

In 1958 Ailey formed the Alvin Ailey American Dance Theater. Most of its members were African Americans, like Ailey. One of the company's early performances was a work by Ailey called *Revelations*. The dance is set to American **Negro spirituals**, and it has become the company's most popular work.

Since the 1960s Ailey's company has performed around the United States and the world. Its popularity made Ailey one of the most famous American choreographers in the world and encouraged people everywhere to appreciate and enjoy modern dance.

Alvin Ailey died in 1989, but the Alvin Ailey American Dance Theater continues to **flourish**. And just as Ailey hoped, the company he founded has expanded from a troupe of mostly black performers to a rich multi-ethnic mix.

SEARCH LIGHT

Ailey began his professional dancing in
a) the 1950s.
b) the 1940s.
c) the 1980s.

LEARN MORE! READ THESE ARTICLES...
COUNT BASIE (VOLUME 4)
NEW YORK CITY, U.S.: THE GREAT CULTURE MART (VOLUME 9)
MARIA TALLCHIEF (VOLUME 3)

Alvin Ailey's dance *Revelations* is the company's signature piece. Since it is set to the religious music of his childhood, the name is quite appropriate. Revelation is the name of the last book of the Christian New Testament.

© Hulton-Deutsch Collection/Corbis

DID YOU KNOW?
Ailey choreographed 79 ballets during his lifetime. Altogether, however, the Alvin Ailey American Dance Theater has performed over 170 works created by more than 65 choreographers.

Answer: b) the 1940s.

DID YOU KNOW?
Bernhardt liked to keep her fans entertained and shocked, so she let it be known that she slept in a coffin every night. Though she slept mostly in an ordinary bed, she did pose for photographs 'asleep' in her coffin.

'The Divine Sarah'

Sarah Bernhardt, called 'the Divine Sarah' by playwright Oscar Wilde, was one of the greatest French actresses of the 19th century - and one of the most famous actresses of all time.

In 1861, at age 17, Bernhardt was enrolled in the acting course at the Paris Conservatoire. She admired some of her teachers. But she considered the school's methods too old-fashioned. Through a family friend, Bernhardt was accepted into the national theatre company, the Comédie-Française. But she soon had to leave because she slapped a senior actress who had been rude to her younger sister. After a period when she questioned her talent for acting, Bernhardt joined the Odéon theatre and, in six years, established her reputation as an actress.

Sarah Bernhardt in the title role of Victorien Sardou's play *Theodora*.
© Hulton-Deutsch Collection/Corbis

Building on her success, Bernhardt returned to the Comédie-Française. When she played the title role in Jean Racine's *Phédre*, she surprised the critics with the passion of her performance and was given excellent reviews. From that point on, she was a star. She performed in France and internationally. And she was in demand for new plays by major writers of the day, as well as for classics such as William Shakespeare's works. She even played a number of male roles, including Hamlet.

Bernhardt possessed a wide emotional range and could show sensitive detail in her acting. Her grace, striking looks, and charm gave her a **commanding** stage **presence**. And her unique voice was sometimes described as sounding like a 'golden bell'. Her popularity also increased because of her dramatic personality offstage.

In 1915 an earlier injury worsened and her right leg had to be removed. She continued to act, however, playing parts she could perform while seated.

LEARN MORE! READ THESE ARTICLES...
JUDI DENCH (VOLUME 3) • PARIS, FRANCE (VOLUME 6)
WILLIAM SHAKESPEARE (VOLUME 4)

SEARCH LIGHT

Why do you think Sarah Bernhardt was nicknamed 'the Divine Sarah'?

Poster of Sarah Bernhardt from the early 1900s.
© Historical Picture Archive/Corbis

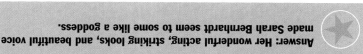

Answer: Her wonderful acting, striking looks, and beautiful voice made Sarah Bernhardt seem to some like a goddess.

A Commanding Actress

Dame Judi Dench is one of England's most famous and admired actresses.

Judith Olivia Dench was born in 1934. In 1957 she had her professional stage **debut** as Hamlet's love, Ophelia, in William Shakespeare's play *Hamlet*. Her performance and delivery were delicate but intelligent, and the character came alive for audiences.

Although a fairly small woman, Dench has always been known for her **commanding** presence onstage. She has acted with the Royal Shakespeare Company and other major theatres. Dench has also played modern roles during her stage career. She created the role of the odd but lovable Sally Bowles in the first London production of the musical *Cabaret* (1968). But Shakespeare has been her specialty.

Outside Great Britain, people probably know Dench best for her role as the stern spy chief 'M' in the James Bond movies. In 1997 the film *Mrs. Brown* brought her wide international attention. She played Queen Victoria in that film. In 1998 she played another queen, Queen Elizabeth I, in the film *Shakespeare in Love*. For this she won an Academy Award for best supporting actress. She won the same award from the British Academy of Film and Television Arts (BAFTA) - one of many she was awarded.

The great strength that Dench communicates has marked her acting style. In addition, however, she gives touchingly personal life to the characters she plays, whether they are grand historical figures or everyday people. Her two popular television series, 'A Fine Romance' and 'As Time Goes By', show off her skill at playing ordinary women.

Judi Dench has always considered the stage her first love. For her remarkable contribution to theatre and films, Dench was honoured with a knighthood as Dame Commander of the British Empire in 1988.

DID YOU KNOW?

Dame Judi Dench's first appearance onstage was as a snail in a production at the Mount School.

LEARN MORE! READ THESE ARTICLES...

In 1994 Judi Dench played the actress Irina Arkadina in the classic Russian play *The Seagull*, written by Anton Chekhov.
© Robbie Jack/Corbis

Answer: Dame Judi Dench has made a number of films and some TV programs, but her greatest love is the stage (or theatre).

DID YOU KNOW?
Kermit the Frog's original eyes were made from a Ping-Pong ball cut in half.

Muppet Master

As a puppeteer and creator of the Muppets, Jim Henson delighted, entertained, and educated several generations of children and adults.

Henson was born in Mississippi, U.S., in 1936. He grew up in Washington, D.C., and began his career as a puppeteer while in secondary school there. Later he and his wife had a short puppet show on local television called 'Sam and Friends'. While he was still in university, Henson put together a team of puppeteers who performed in commercials and on TV.

Jim Henson's granddaughters Katrina (left) and Virginia Henson with Kermit the Frog when he was given his own star on the Hollywood Walk of Fame in 2002.
© Reuters Newmedia Inc./Corbis

In 1969 the Children's Television Workshop created a TV show with Henson called 'Sesame Street'. The program featured his 'Muppets' and included such now well-known characters as Kermit the Frog, Grover, Big Bird, and Cookie Monster. Young viewers loved the Muppets. But 'Sesame Street' also proved Henson's belief that learning could be fun.

The Muppets are a unique form of puppetry that was new to television. Often it takes two people to operate a Muppet since the head and each arm may require a human hand to move them. The larger Muppets, like Snuffleupagus and Big Bird, are actually costumed actors. The puppeteer who controls each Muppet also provides the character's voice. Henson operated and voiced Kermit himself for 35 years.

'Sesame Street' was so successful that in 1976 Henson created 'The Muppet Show' - a TV programme for both adults and children. The Muppets have appeared in several films as well, including *The Muppet Movie* and *Muppets from Space*.

Sadly, Henson died suddenly of pneumonia in 1990. But his Muppets continue to perform today, with Henson's son Brian leading the company.

LEARN MORE! READ THESE ARTICLES...
FOLK ARTS AND CRAFTS (VOLUME 3) • FROGS (VOLUME 11)
THEATRE (VOLUME 3)

SEARCH LIGHT

Henson's first TV show was called
a) 'Cheers'.
b) 'Sam and Friends'.
c) 'The Banana Bunch'.

Jim Henson, seen here among some of his Muppets, was a favourite with both children and adults. Some adults enjoyed Henson's work from the time they were children themselves.

Answer: b) 'Sam and Friends'.

A Vision in Motion

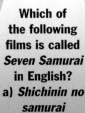

SEARCH LIGHT

Which of the following films is called *Seven Samurai* in English?
a) *Shichinin no samurai*
b) *Yoidore tenshi*
c) *Ikiru*

Film-maker Akira Kurosawa got his start working as an assistant director for a Japanese film studio. In 1943 he wrote and directed his first feature film, *Sanshiro Sugata*. The story of 19th-century **judo** masters became very popular with Japanese audiences.

Kurosawa's fame grew in 1948 with his film *Yoidore tenshi* (*Drunken Angel*). The film is about an alcoholic doctor who helps the poor fight against disease and **gangsters**. It stars Toshiro Mifune, who appeared in most of Kurosawa's films. In 1951 *Rashomon* made Kurosawa the first world-famous Japanese film-maker. The film won the Grand Prix at the Venice Film Festival and the Academy Award for best foreign film.

Many consider Kurosawa's best film to be *Ikiru* (*To Live*), from 1952. It follows a man who has only a few months to live and spends his last days helping the poor. Two

Kurosawa with American directors Francis Ford Coppola and George Lucas.
© The Kobal Collection—Toho/Kurosawa

Kurosawa's film *Ran* ('Chaos') is felt by many to be his finest work. It is a version of Shakespeare's play *King Lear* set in 16th-century Japan.

© The Kobal Collection/Herald Ace-Nippon—Herald-Greenwich

years later Kurosawa released his most popular film: *Shichinin no samurai* (*Seven Samurai*). The film is a **tribute** to American westerns - but with **samurai** warriors instead of cowboys. In fact, it was later remade in the United States as the western *The Magnificent Seven*.

Many of Kurosawa's films were set in historical Japan. But his work was popular in Japan and throughout the world. It combined artistic ideas, emotions, and images with plenty of action and drama to keep viewers entertained.

Kurosawa died in 1998. The Kurosawa Akira **Memorial** Satellite Studio has been opened on the Japanese island of Kyushu. It was there that he filmed several of his masterpieces, including *Ran* and *Kagemusha*.

LEARN MORE! READ THESE ARTICLES...
JAPAN: MODERN NATION OF ANCIENT TRADITIONS (VOLUME 7)
MOTION PICTURES (VOLUME 2) • SATYAJIT RAY (VOLUME 3)

Answer: a) *Shichinin no samurai*

Satyajit Ray's 1977 film *Shatranj ke Khilari* (in English, *The Chess Players*) was his first one made in the Hindi language. It deals with the effect of the West on India.
© Nimai Ghosh

DID YOU KNOW?

Because Ray had so little money for his first movie, his film crew worked for free. This seemed all right, since none of the crew had ever worked on a film before.

Indian Cinema for the World

Satyajit Ray is probably India's best-known film director and screenwriter. His sensitive and visually interesting works let the world see Indian cinema as more than simple entertainment.

Ray was born in Calcutta, India, in 1921. He started out working as an illustrator for books and advertising. At one point he illustrated the Bengali novel *Pather Panchali* - in

English, *The Song of the Road.* It tells the story of Apu, the poor son of a priest. Apu wants to be a novelist and travels from his small village to the city of Calcutta. The story shows the conflict between traditional and modern life.

Satyajit Ray.
© Camera Press

SEARCH LIGHT

How did Ray start out?
a) as an illustrator
b) as a writer
c) as a director

Ray was interested in making a film of *Pather Panchali.* And a famous French director, Jean Renoir, encouraged him. Ray started work on the film in 1952, using friends as actors and film crew. He at first used his own money, but the West Bengal government eventually supplied the rest.

Ray completed the film in 1955. It was a tremendous success. *Pather Panchali* won a major award at the 1956 Cannes International Film Festival. After this, Ray became a very popular and respected film-maker.

Most of his films are about the struggles of poor people. They also focus on the challenges of the modern world. Ray made all kinds of films: comedies, tragedies, romances, musicals, and detective stories. All of his films, however, show his insight into how people behave and what they go through.

Ray also wrote many short stories and books. But he is best remembered as the person who woke up the world to the possibilities of fine filmmaking in India.

LEARN MORE! READ THESE ARTICLES...
CINEMA (VOLUME 3) • INDIA (VOLUME 7) • AKIRA KUROSAWA (VOLUME 3)

Answer: a) as an illustrator

DID YOU KNOW?

Maria's sister, Marjorie Tallchief, was a successful ballerina as well. She was the first American to become a lead dancer with the Paris Opéra Ballet. And she and Maria worked together many times over the years.

America's Prima Ballerina

Delicate, **effortlessly** graceful, radiant, and enchanting - that is how Maria Tallchief has been described. Many people consider her America's finest ballerina ever.

Maria Tallchief was born in 1925, in the small town of Fairfax, Oklahoma. She spent the first eight years of her life in northeastern Oklahoma. Her father was a member of the Osage tribe of American Indians. Her mother was of Irish and Scottish **descent**.

Tallchief enjoyed the Osage ceremonial dances. She loved music and dancing. She trained as a pianist but her heart was in dancing.

When her family moved to Los Angeles, she studied dance. One of Tallchief's teachers, dancer Bronislava Nijinska, was strict. She always

Tallchief receiving National Medal of Arts from President Bill Clinton in 1999.
AP/Wide World Photos

said, 'When you sleep, sleep like a ballerina. Even on the street waiting for a bus, stand like a ballerina'.

Tallchief worked hard for five years and then joined the Ballet Russe de Monte Carlo. She danced in many ballets and even gave solo performances. Some of these solos were in *Scheherazade* and **choreographer** George Balanchine's *Serenade* and *Firebird*.

Tallchief married Balanchine in 1946, and soon they were both working with the company that became the New York City Ballet. Tallchief was so popular that she had to give as many as eight performances in a week! She was the prima ballerina (main female dancer) with NYCB for most of the next 20 years.

In 1953 she was honoured as America's 'Woman of the Year'. That same year her home state of Oklahoma honoured her achievements and her Native American identity by naming her Wa-Xthe-Thomba, meaning 'Woman of Two Worlds'.

Tallchief retired from dancing in 1965. She felt it was time to pass on to young dancers what she had learned about the art that she loved.

LEARN MORE! READ THESE ARTICLES...
DANCE (VOLUME 3) • FANNY ELSSLER (VOLUME 4) • AMERICAN INDIAN (VOLUME 4)

Maria Tallchief's dancing in *Firebird* became her most famous work.
© Hulton-Deutsch Collection/Corbis

Answer: b) Woman of the Year

New Zealand's Opera Star

Kiri Te Kanawa was born in 1944 in New Zealand. At the age of 5 weeks, she was adopted. Her adoptive and biological mothers were both of British descent. Her adoptive and biological fathers were Maori (native New Zealanders).

Te Kanawa's mother discovered very early that her daughter was musical. So her parents sent her to a school where a well-known singer taught music. After leaving school Te Kanawa won various singing competitions in New Zealand and Australia.

By the 1970s Te Kanawa was world famous as a **soprano** diva (leading female vocalist) of opera. Her first big success was in Wolfgang Amadeus Mozart's opera *The Marriage of Figaro*. She performed in many Mozart operas after that.

Te Kanawa made her first appearance at the Metropolitan Opera in New York City quite by accident. The lead star playing Desdemona in Giuseppe Verdi's *Otello* suddenly fell ill. Te Kanawa was asked to perform instead, with only three hours to rehearse! She did such a splendid job that everyone raved about her performance.

In 1981 Te Kanawa sang at the wedding of Britain's Prince Charles and Princess Diana. She sang George Frideric Handel's 'Let the Bright

Te Kanawa filming a video.
© Le Poer Trench Michael—Sygma/Corbis

Seraphim'. This performance was seen on television by millions of viewers all over the world.

Te Kanawa is particularly known for the warmth of her soprano voice and her engaging personality on the stage. She has made a number of recordings. Most of these are of classical pieces, but she has also recorded traditional Maori songs from her New Zealand childhood.

In 1982 Te Kanawa was given a British noble title. She was made Dame Kiri Te Kanawa for the joy her singing had brought to so many.

LEARN MORE! READ THESE ARTICLES…

NEW ZEALAND (VOLUME 7) • OPERA (VOLUME 3)
JOAN SUTHERLAND (VOLUME 4)

Dame Kiri Te Kanawa appears here in Richard Strauss's comedic opera *Arabella*.
© Robbie Jack/Corbis

DID YOU KNOW?
In 1990, during a tour of Australia and New Zealand, Kiri Te Kanawa performed at an outdoor concert in the city of Auckland. An audience of 140,000 people attended.

Answer: FALSE. She is a soprano.

GLOSSARY

abstract (adjective) artistically communicating feelings or ideas about a subject, rather than creating a realistic image

acrylic type of paint

affordable reasonable in price

archaeology (adjective: archaeological) the science that deals with past human life as shown by fossils, tools, and other material left by ancient peoples

archbishop high-ranking churchman in some Christian churches who supervises church government in a very large area

blockbuster huge, successful event

cast to form a shape by pouring a liquid into a mould and letting it harden

choreographer creator of a dance

civil war war between opposing groups of citizens of the same country

classical traditional in style

commanding grand and powerful

commission (verb) to order to be made; (noun) an order granting the power to perform various acts or duties

compose to create a work of art

composition literary, musical, or other artistic work

conductor the leader of an orchestra

conquistador (plural: conquistadores) a Spanish conqueror of Latin America

critic person who studies and comments on the quality of performances or works of art

dean head of a division of a school or university

debut first formal public appearance

depict to represent by a picture

descent ancestry, heritage, or origin

dialogue conversation in a play, film, or written work

dictate to speak for another person to write down or for a machine to record

effortless easy and natural

energetic lively or active

expression communication, usually of emotions or ideas

fantastical highly imaginative and unrealistic

fibre strand or thread-like structure

flourish to grow successfully; to do well

formal following a specific order or pattern

fresco painting done on freshly spread moist plaster

fusion the blending or combination of two or more things, as if melted together

gangster member of a gang of criminals

gospel, or **gospel music** black American music that grew mostly from Christian church services, blues, and traditional spirituals

humanitarian devoted to the happiness and welfare of other people

hymn song of joy or praise, often to a god

industrialized built up and modernized through business and manufacturing

industry business and manufacturing

integrate (adjective: integrated) to combine two or more parts in order to create a more balanced whole; *especially*, to remove barriers that isolate one group of people from another

intricate complicated or detailed

ivory material that makes up elephant and walrus tusks

judo sport, developed from the Japanese fighting art of *jujitsu*, in which opponents use quick movements and careful positioning to try to throw each other to the ground

landscape picture showing views of nature and the countryside

lyrics the words of a song

majestic grand or splendid

memorial something that keeps alive the memory of a person or event

mourn to feel great sorrow, usually because of a death or other loss

mural a painting on a wall

Negro spiritual religious folk song developed among blacks in the southern United States

orchestra group of musicians playing together, usually with a leader called a 'conductor'

pastel type of drawing crayon

poet laureate poet honoured by a country or other region as its most outstanding poet

political having to do with creating and controlling a government

portray to show by making a picture or by imitating; also, to act the part of a character in a play

presence the strong and self-confident quality a person has that makes others focus on him or her

print (noun) work of art made by a process that allows more than one copy of an image to be made

recycle to reuse, or to pass used or scrap material through various changes in order to create new useful products from it

refined polished, complex, and advanced

revolution (adjective: revolutionary) activity or movement designed to make changes in a situation

rhythm (adjective: rhythmic) regular pattern of sound

samurai warrior class in Japan from about the 12th to the mid-19th century

science fiction stories that deal with the effects of real or imagined science on society or individuals

score in films, the background music that goes with the pictures on the screen

sculpture three-dimensional artwork, usually shaped by carving, moulding, or welding

self-portrait picture of a person, usually showing the face, that is painted or drawn by the artist himself or herself

seraphim in Christianity, Islam, and Judaism, special angels who guard God's throne

shrine place where honour or worship is offered to a saint or deity

slum crowded, dirty, run-down housing

soprano the highest woman's singing voice; also, a person who sings in this voice

stylized simplified or made to suggest natural forms but not imitate them

superstition unproven belief usually based on a mistaken idea of how something is caused

symbolize to stand for something else; *especially*, to stand for or suggest something that cannot itself be pictured or shown

technical having to do with the way a skilled individual handles the details of an art or craft

technology scientific ideas and knowledge put to actual use

texture the feel of a surface

theme the main idea or subject of a work of art; *especially*, in music, the main melody that a piece of music builds on

three-dimensional having depth (or thickness), in addition to width and height

translation version of a written work that has been changed from its original language into another

tribute gift, performance, or action meant to show appreciation, respect, or caring for someone

troupe company or group; *especially*, a working group of stage performers

vaudeville popular American form of entertainment from the 1890s to the 1930s, involving musical, dancing, comedy, magic, and other variety acts

vivid bright or dramatic

weld to join metal parts together with heat

yacht small ship or large boat used for pleasure cruising or racing